MW01181592

about

Life

and how to do it

A **to** Z

smallpage press 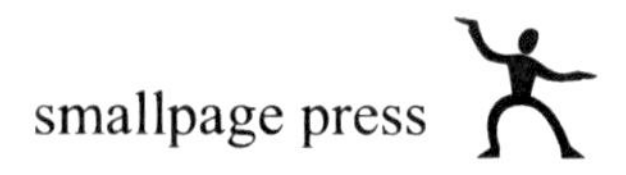

2744 53rd St.
Des Moines, Iowa 50310

10 9 8 7 6 5 4 3 2 1

Printed in the United States of America
November 2014

Library of Congress Control Number: 2014946783

ISBN: 978-1-60047-982-3

Contents

CONTENTS

Introduction

One day many years ago, I walked past a white house with a porch all across the front and green shutters at the windows and stopped to look at furniture spread out in the yard. There were beds and dressers, tables and chairs, boxes of books and rugs, glasses and plates and pots and pans – the many furnishings of a household.

It was the year I was seventeen and on my own for the first time. The only things in the apartment I had rented the day before were a sleeping bag, a table with two crooked legs, a battered straight chair and boxes of clothes and books. I was in immediate need of some furniture.

A man sitting in a wicker rocking chair on the porch seemed to be in charge. I introduced myself and we shook hands. "I'm Horace Hooper," he said. He and his wife were the owners of the house and the furniture. He explained that they were leaving the house where they had lived for 40 years and moving to a smaller place. Everything was for sale. I chose a small wood table at which to eat, three straight chairs – none like the other – a chest of drawers painted white, a bookcase with glass doors that could be pulled down over each shelf, a rug of oriental look, an iron bedstead that came complete with mattress, pillows and a patchwork quilt, a sofa with dark blue velvet upholstery, and a round mirror with a golden tortoiseshell frame. Also a box of books that Mr. Hooper said had belonged to a neighbor, Miss Ida Jacobs, who had moved away and left some things behind. He would see that she got the money for her books.

Then, just as I was ready to leave, I noticed a trunk by the porch steps, nearly hidden under a lilac bush. It had brass corners, a large brass hasp, a flat top, and leather handles on each end. A key was tied with twine to one of the handles. I had no need for a trunk, but I liked its antique look. It was graceful and elegant in a worn way, as though it had traveled around the world and back again and was better for it. I asked the price. "For $2.00 it's yours," said Mr. Hooper. I said I would take it.

Days are full of things that happen – most of them as fleeting as the hours between waking and sleeping – but there are days when something happens, or someone or something shows up, that stays and grows until it is a part of who you are. A small canvas trunk with brass corners, resting under a lilac bush one spring morning, owner unknown, has stayed with me all the years since.

With the help of a friend I moved my purchases to my apartment and that night I sat down to inspect the trunk. It was locked, so I cut the twine, turned the key in the lock and lifted the lid. Inside, neatly folded, were the necessaries of a man's life in days gone by. There were two pairs of men's wool pants – navy blue – four white linen shirts with banded collars, socks, underwear, a pair of leather shoes with high tops and a heavy wool coat with a wide collar and deep pockets. Under the clothes in an oval frame was a photograph of a young man. On the back of the photograph was written: "With love to all, Paul." Beneath the photograph was a leather portfolio and under everything was a small wooden box wrapped in a piece of blue linen. In the box was a wide gold ring with the inscription "Pure Gold", a dried pink rose still holding its perfect shape, and a snapshot of a woman walking beside a house, carrying something.

The man in the photograph was wearing a coat, a vest, a bow tie and a shirt with a high stiff-looking collar. His hair was straight and thick and his gaze direct. There was something deep and thoughtful about the look in his eyes, as though he had just said something and was waiting for a reply. He looked like someone's favorite brother who had gone off to war or been lost at sea – someone never to forget.

These things, gathered together and neatly packed, had once belonged to someone and perhaps had been put away in love and remembrance. I wanted to keep the trunk but thought I should offer to return the contents, so the next day I returned to the site of the sale and found Mr. Hooper sitting in his rocking chair on the porch, just as he had been the day before. Greeting him, I told of my discovery and offered to return the clothes and photographs and papers. Looking over the top of his glasses he said, in a voice that was a bit gruff, "That trunk was in the attic when we bought the house. You're welcome to it and what's in it. It's yours to keep, no strings." I assured him that I was happy with my new possessions, and after chatting about the state of the world, the weather and the possibility of rain, we parted.

One night, several weeks later, I sat down and began to read the papers in the portfolio. It was full, stuffed really, with sheets of paper covered in very small handwriting. Parts of some pages were cut off with another piece of paper fastened on with straight pins. On some pages the writing climbed the side of the page and went over the top and down the other side. Some pages were numbered and some were not, and there seemed to be an effort to write pieces beginning with a letter of the alphabet. A page would begin with a large letter "D" and be continued on another page that was fastened to a page that began with "E". Some letters occurred more than once and some not at all. And there were pages with thoughts that had no connection to letters of the alphabet.

The more I read the more I wondered who the writer had been. It was like reading mystery novel when you can't stop reading because you wonder how it is going to end and "who done it." Was the photograph of the writer and was his name Paul? If so, was the work done when he was young, or middle aged or even old? Or could the work have been learned from someone else and written down from memory? And who was in the snapshot walking beside a house, why was the rose saved and whose ring was it? I tried on the shirts and pants, and they fit almost perfectly. The shoes were a bit too big.

The more I read, the more real the author seemed real to me, as real as anyone I knew and nearly as real as the family I came from. My family, two by two and one by one, had gone to places so far away

I could not reach them. All of my grandparents died before I was old enough to remember them. And one winter day, driving home from Des Moines, my parents' car hit an icy spot on the pavement and slid into a row of trees. The car was smashed and my parents killed. In those days there were no seat belts or air bags and if your car crashed you were pretty much out of luck. After that, my brother and I were orphans.

My Uncle Beau, my father's brother, took us in to live with him and we settled into a new way of being, but it wasn't long before Beau went to a convention in Kansas City and met a woman from England, fell in love, married her, and decided to move to England. This was two years after my mother's sister moved to Australia. Beau and my new Aunt Thelma invited us to go with them and live in England. My brother decided to go. I decided not to. This is how it happened that I was buying furniture at a yard sale when I was seventeen, and how I acquired the possessions and thoughts of a man I would never know.

Beau didn't want to leave me behind, but I was stubborn and thought I knew almost everything there was to know. In those days I was filled with confidence and fear. Some days the confidence beat back the fear and other days the fear overwhelmed the confidence. When I was troubled or confused, I often pulled out a few pages from the portfolio and read a bit. After a time, I began to think of the man in the photograph who had signed his name on the back, "With love to all, Paul", as the author, and I consulted him often. It was like having a wise uncle at my disposal, but one who couldn't tell me what to do or criticize me. I couldn't talk back, but I didn't need to. I could just put the papers away and close the trunk.

I went to school, got a job, and then another job. I put the trunk beside my bed, and with a lamp on top it made a fine bedside table. The contents of the trunk were still a jumble ten years later when I met Sara and our life together began. One day Sara asked what was in the trunk, and I showed her the clothes, the box, the photograph and the portfolio. She unfolded the clothes, shook them out, folded them back and began to read the papers in the portfolio. When she had read everything several times, she announced that the writer was an excellent thinker but very disorganized. She wondered if his work had been interrupted and his life cut short by illness or accident. We could only wonder. There was no way to know. The things and thoughts we found in the trunk that now belonged to us had no story to go with them.

After a time, Sara decided to put the writer's work into organized form, sorting out the various thoughts and connecting those that belonged together. She was quite sure he would have done so had he not run out of time. Off and on for many years, she worked on organizing the papers. She made some additions until each letter of the alphabet had a thought to match, and she found illustrations to add to them making, as she said, "a regular book." By circumstance – or luck – the trunk and everything in it now belonged to us to use as we wished.

The writer, long gone from the world, owes Sara for bringing his work from darkness and incompleteness to light, and we owe him for what he has taught us and the help he has given us. I offer here the work that Sara put together – twenty-six thoughts arranged from A to Z – about living in this amazing world.

Sometimes things come together in ways we have not imagined and surprise us, or wake us up, or do both, and so it is for Sara and me. We never knew the young man who until now was gone from life and memory, but we hold him in our hearts as dearly as if we had. One year in April, when lilacs bloomed, I bought a trunk and it made all the difference.

Sam Maitree

We use words to think.

LIFE IS AN AMAZING ADVENTURE

There is an old story about how amazing it is to be born on this earth. It says, imagine there is a turtle on the bottom of a vast sea and that one day, seeking light and air, this turtle rises to the surface of the water. Then imagine that floating somewhere on the surface of the sea is a wooden ring and that the turtle comes to the surface right through the middle of that wooden ring. This is how amazing it is that you – by chance – came to be.

To be here on this earth is amazing. To see, to hear, to touch, to know, to taste and smell, to love and be loved is a wonder, and the earth is a wonder. Viewed from space it looks like a bright, shining marble in utter blackness. But we who live here know it is a place of light and dark, life and death, a place full of creatures great and small living in mysterious cooperation. Looking out in space as far as we can see, there is nothing like it.

We ask, "Why has the earth come to be? Why am I here, and what am I supposed to do while I'm here?" The birds that fly can't ask these questions, or the fish that swim in the sea, or the trees that bend in the wind. But we can.

The answer is: we are the searchers, the watchers, the learners and the caretakers. We are here to care for the world and for each other and to add goodness to the world.

The world is a gift. Receive it as a gift and give back.

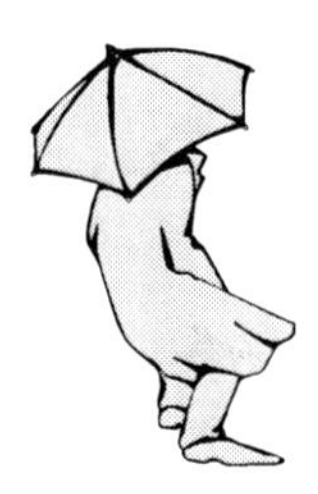

Get started. Watch your step. Keep on going.

WHATEVER HAPPENS BELIEVE IN YOURSELF

Believe in yourself no matter what your faults are, and care for the world no matter how good or bad it seems to be. Be proud of what you have done and humble for how much you have yet to learn and do.

Stand up for yourself and for your rights but respect the rights of others. Believing in yourself doesn't mean you have the right to grab from others or take what doesn't belong to you.

Don't knowingly harm another person.

Disappointments and setbacks discourage us. We make mistakes. We begin but often stumble and feel embarrassed or ashamed. No one can be perfect.

You aren't as good as you want to be – that's OK – just keep on getting better.

Act as though what you do matters... because it does.

You are in the world to keep it running and make it better. If you want to cheat the world, don't take care of yourself.

What you do in this world may not make the history books, but it will matter, more than you will ever know.

CARE FOR YOUR BODY – YOU ONLY GET ONE

Give your body good food and clean water and keep it clean. Listen to it; rest when you are tired. Search out beautiful things to see and hear. If you don't choose what you see and hear, others will, and their motives may not be the best.

As much as possible, be positive. Much worry comes from thinking that the worst is sure to happen and from fearing that you can do nothing to prevent it. But the worst is only one possible outcome and not always – but almost always – you can do something to change things for the better.

If illness strikes, seek out the best medical help: outside help may be needed. If it is a serious condition, get more than one opinion.

Your body has a natural ability to heal, but if you push it beyond reasonable limits, it won't work well or may stop working.

Nature gives a natural punishment for excess.

When you treat someone well you won't always get good treatment in return. Don't let that stop you from doing what is right.

TREAT OTHERS DECENTLY

Treat people decently even if you don't like them, are mad at them, or don't agree with them. Everyone, no matter what he or she has done or looks like, has the right to go about life with a point of view and with self-respect. Those who disregard the rules and laws of the community may deserve a penalty under law, but they have the right to be treated decently and fairly. Not that you have to be terrifically polite to everyone, just be decent.

Not that being polite is always easy. It can be tempting to insult others when their beliefs and ways of being aren't the same as yours. It helps to remember that human beings have a sense of self that doesn't like being treated rudely. If you insult others, sooner or later you will likely get insults in return. Treating others decently is not only an ethical choice, it can save you a lot of trouble.

There will be times when people will be rude to you, and you will feel like giving it back. You may think, "If he can do it, why can't I?" This is where you really get tested. If you keep on being polite, even when you are treated rudely, you win. If you don't, you lose because giving rude treatment back lets another person determine your behavior.

When you have no choice but to interact with disagreeable or unreliable people, keep to your own standards and be on guard that your feelings don't take over. You lose if you lose your cool. (But you can always get it back.)

Everyone has a mean streak, some have only a little, others a lot. However much you have to start with, you probably will feel like giving hurt back many times. Keep checking on your own mean streak and making it smaller. Eventually you'll find you don't much need it.

Giving place to others without losing one's own position

is one secret of success in this world.

You will meet people who flatter you and say you are wonderful, not because they really think so but to get you to do what they want. And you will meet bullies who criticize you so you will try to get their approval or do as they say. (Flatterers and bullies are a lot alike.) If your feelings aren't affected by flatterers and bullies who try to manipulate you, then you can escape their power.

But if someone is about to hurt you or put you in danger, you can stop being polite. Protect yourself when necessary. This may mean no more than saying no to an invitation, or it could mean walking away, running away, or ending a relationship. It may mean getting help. And sometimes, to protect yourself, you have to strike back.

Try not to swim where there are sharks.

Keep your balance.

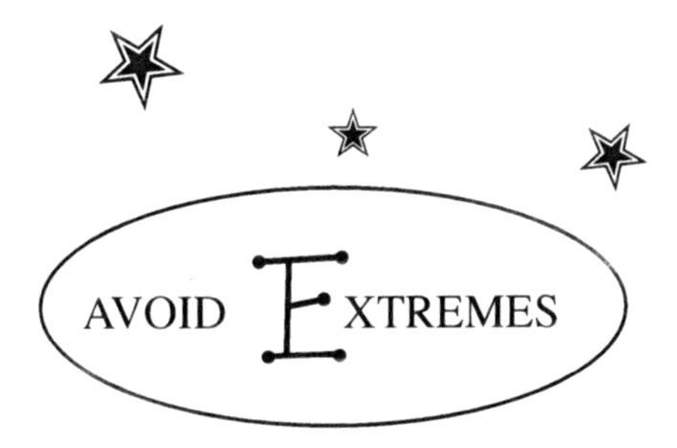

Too much is an extreme and so is too little. Neither is good. Almost always, the middle way is best.

> If you eat too much you will get fat. If you eat too little you will be undernourished or starve.
>
> If you spend all your money, you will be broke, but if you hide your money away and spend nothing, you will be a miserable miser.
>
> If you drive too fast on the highway, you may cause an accident or get a ticket. If you drive too slow – same thing.
>
> Too much bravery is recklessness. Too little bravery is cowardice.
>
> You lose if you don't stick with anything, but if you stick with something that isn't working out or that wasn't good to start with, you also may lose.

The human world keeps wobbling out of balance, going from one extreme to another. Avoid extremes and you will help the world.

Not to have feelings is inhuman.
To be carried away by feelings is foolish.

YOU CAN'T HELP YOUR FEELINGS BUT YOU CAN HELP HOW YOU ACT

Feelings just show up without being invited, and once they show up they have a way of trying to get us to do something about them, like saying something nasty or hurting someone. If feelings take over, there can be a lot of trouble – trouble that can be avoided if you know how.

Whether you feel angry, fearful, resentful, ashamed, grateful, or loving, or have any other feeling, it's up to you whether or not to express what you feel. There's an old saying, "Count to ten before you speak." In other words, take time to apply reason to your feelings; before you speak or act... think. (Maybe count to twenty or thirty.)

You can act on your feelings, but you don't have to. You can keep quiet and do nothing, or you can say something or do something.

It's impossible not to have feelings, but you can control what you do with them. And remember: having a feeling and acting on it are not the same. There's a lot of difference between feeling like hitting someone and actually doing it. And don't feel guilty for the feelings you have, even though they're invisible, they're real.

Actions have consequences that feelings don't.

A rose bush has flowers and thorns, so does life.

WHERE DOES GOODNESS COME FROM?

Some good comes from the earth. With energy from the sun, the earth grows plants for us and for animals. The earth gives us air, water, mighty oceans, majestic mountains, deep rivers and fertile plains. Formed through eons of time, it is a living, growing thing that shines in beauty and mystery.

It also gives us earthquakes, hurricanes, tornados and floods that harm and destroy.

Good also comes from human beings. Through the years, people have given effort to understanding and improving the world. They have invented, explored and discovered. They have bred animals and plants to increase the supply of food, made music, poetry, paintings and sculpture, and built beautiful buildings. They wondered about the meaning of life and learned that the human spirit can survive and soar even when there is pain, suffering and loss, and they have kept the world going by working away at everyday chores. Their work and thought live on in us.

People also have been – and sometimes now are – cruel and destructive. They have made war to oppress others, killed millions, ruined cities, burned the land, and given privilege to themselves, taking more than their fair share. They have chosen to control those close to them and do harmful, even evil, things.

Circumstance – sometimes called luck – can bring either good or evil. We can increase our chances of having good luck by being prepared and by being in the right place at the right time, or we can avoid bad luck by staying away from some places, but many things in life are not in our control, and luck is one of them. Life doesn't choose which person to favor, just as the earth doesn't choose to make storms and cause earthquakes.

If you don't control your desires, they will control you.

As far as we know, only human beings have the power to choose between actions that are mean, violent and selfish or those that are generous, constructive, life-loving and that benefit the human community.

However, knowing how to choose what is good doesn't come naturally, the way children learn to walk without being taught. We have to ***learn*** the difference between good and evil. And at the beginning of our lives, when we have to start making choices before we have enough experience to make wise ones, we must borrow from the experience of others. We learn from our parents and the people around us and from wise and thoughtful people, some living and some who have lived before. We learn from what they say and what they have written.

It is also possible to learn bad values if we have bad models.

After we learn the difference between good and evil comes the hardest part, because then we have to learn self-control. When we feel like striking out at others, not caring for ourselves, ignoring the law, cheating, or saying something nasty – and anyone who says he or she never feels this way isn't telling the truth – we can choose instead to do what is unselfish, kind, decent, honest and caring.

Maybe choosing self-control is the most important choice we ever make, because goodness is impossible without it.

Making sense of life takes time.

When we are honest, we hold up the civilized world.

BE HONEST

When people aren't honest – when they lie, steal, cheat and harm others – there is chaos. Why would anyone work if they thought that what they earned could be grabbed away from them anytime? If everyone wrote bad checks, if the banks did not return the money you deposited, if people lied, stole and injured others without penalty, most goodness would disappear from the world.

Nearly every day there are stories in the news about people who cheat others or steal from them. Some are fined or put in jail, but not all get caught. The fact is, some people get away with being dishonest, but both those who get away with it and those who are caught have harmed others.

Every group of people must have rules and laws that put forth standards of acceptable behavior, as well as punishment for not following rules and laws. Things keep getting worse in a town, city, county, state or country where there aren't laws that protect the rights of individuals or where laws can't be enforced. Without laws, individuals try to gain for themselves without regard to the rights of others. Some use force to get power over others, many become thieves and some harm – even kill – others.

Do your part by being honest in all you do – in school, at work, and in all your relationships. Pay your bills on time and be a good neighbor and friend. Don't trick or fool other people.

Tell the truth as you know it but with kindness. Some facts should not be spoken for your sake or for the sake of someone else; you don't have to tell everything you know or think. It's not lying to turn a question away with a polite, non-committal answer.

Watch out for people who use words to get your feelings riled up.

When you are asked a question that you don't want to answer or that isn't anyone's business (unless you are in a situation of law), and you don't want to lie, smile (be sure to smile) and in a pleasant tone say something like, "No comment," or "I'd rather not say," or "Who knows?" and change the subject. If someone persists and asks again, repeat what you said.

Keep on being polite even when someone is persistently nosey. Some may take offense at not getting an answer, but your privacy is more valuable than their approval.

Don't be naive. Not everyone has good intentions.

Time is free, but it is priceless.

INVEST YOUR TIME WELL

It may seem strange to think of time as something in which to invest, but time, talent and health are the basic materials we have to work with in life. We have only so much time to do the things we want to do and to make a difference for ourselves and for the world. If we waste time, we waste part of our basic wealth, and when time is wasted, it is gone forever. (Not that we should work every minute we are awake. Recreation and relaxation are important investments in ourselves.)

It is up to each of us to figure out how to spend our time, but there are a few general rules:

First, be realistic about how much time something will take. Some things can be done quickly, and some can't. You can't walk 500 miles in a day or become a concert pianist overnight. So start early and allow more time than you think you will need.

Second, success comes from experience. Get started and keep at it. Practice will make you better.

Third, some things can be done at one time and not another. If you plant seeds in November in Iowa, they won't grow because winter is about to start. If you plan to paint the garage on your vacation but put it off until the last day and it rains all day, you can't follow your plan because you didn't take time into consideration. Don't procrastinate (too much).

And fourth, when you are to be someplace at a certain time, for work or an appointment, allow extra time and be a little early. But if you are going to someone's house, be on time or a few minutes

It's good to have the best cards at the table. It's also good to know when it's time to get up and leave.

late. It is as rude to be early when you go to visit as it is to be late.

Not everyone is reliable about doing things when they need to be done. By messing with time they frustrate and control others. (This may be the idea.) If you choose to live with someone who is not reliable about time, or don't have a choice but to live with him or her, you most likely will feel frustrated and angry. But don't expect someone who is unreliable about time to change, even when you point it out.

Give time to school, work, family and friends. But save some time for yourself to think, dream, write, or pursue a hobby. Be an expert or an amateur: keep on learning.

Sometimes rest with a clear mind and let time stand still.

It's foolish never to laugh and foolish to laugh at serious things.

JOKE AND LAUGH BUT DON'T LAUGH AT SERIOUS THINGS

We laugh when things or people are preposterous, and sometimes we laugh at the predicament we are in. Sometimes we laugh and cry at the same time, sometimes we laugh at someone for being so puffed up, sometimes we laugh when we see a truth that is hidden, and sometimes we laugh for sheer happiness. In all of creation, only human beings can do this.

Laugh often but don't laugh at or make fun of others who are close to you. Don't tease, especially don't laugh at or tease a child. Circumstance can do a plenty good job of hurting our feelings, don't add to it by poking fun at those you know.

If you can't be kind, at least do no harm.

Sorrow is a weed, but joy needs tending.

Aim to be liked by people who are honest and reliable.

KEEP GOOD COMPANY

Nothing is more important than choosing good companions. Customs, tastes, beliefs and ways of being are transmitted silently without our being aware of it. We "catch" these things much as we "catch" a germ from others. We even catch moods from others. Be around upbeat people and your spirits will rise, be around sour, gloomy people and your mood will get darker. People leave their mark on us.

Choose friends who are honest, thoughtful, hardworking and who treat others decently. Don't choose friends because they are popular, rich, or good looking if their values aren't the same as yours. Some people mean well but are undisciplined or have low values. Avoid braggarts and complainers and anyone who is mean to others.

Don't go into a relationship before you can judge character; what shows on the outside is often not a true measure of a person. And don't enter into a relationship thinking you can change someone. People can change, but they must want to, and it takes time.

You don't have to take someone for a friend just because he or she wants to be friends. If someone wants to be friends, but you don't, be tactful about responding to invitations and overtures.

Some will try to win your friendship by flattering you, but you don't have to spend time with a flatterer. Others will leave you out or criticize you so that you will try to please them. Be alert to such behavior and don't be fooled. Bullies and flatterers play on your feelings in order to control you. Some day, you may meet someone who flatters you so that you will you rescue them. Help others when you can but don't let anyone turn you into a rescuer.

No company is better than bad company.

Enjoy your acquaintances; be loyal. Listen to them and don't criticize them to others or betray their privacy. Share your thoughts and the events of your day with them, but tell only what you would want everyone in the world to know because what you tell one person everybody will soon know. You tell one person, who will tell someone else, who will tell someone else. Almost no one can keep a secret.

There's goodness and kindness and wisdom in this world,

but it can be hard to find. Keep looking.

Democracy:
Government in which the people hold the ruling power through elected representatives – rule by the ruled.

LAWS PROTECT THE WEAK FROM THE POWERFUL AND THE GOOD FROM THE WICKED

Where do laws come from? In the past, and in some places now, rules and laws were decided by elders, or by the strongest person or by a king who says his power comes from God. But in the United States we have developed a system in which a Constitution sets forth basic principles by which we govern ourselves. Guided by the Constitution, we elect legislators to make laws, and we have people to make sure the laws are followed, such as policemen and sheriffs. We elect judges to make decisions when there is disagreement about the meaning of the law, and we have juries to decide guilt or innocence. In the United States we believe that every person, no matter what he or she has done, has the right to be protected by the law and that anyone accused of a crime and brought to trial is entitled to a lawyer in court, whether the person can pay for a lawyer or not. We believe there should be justice for everyone: the Pledge of Allegiance says, "with liberty and justice for all."

Our system is not perfect. There are some bad laws and some dishonest officials, and not everyone believes in liberty and justice for all. But unless citizens have a part in making laws and in electing the men and women who carry out the law, thugs and bullies and dictators will force people to do what they want them to do. Even in a democratic system such as ours, there are people who advocate violence rather than the rule of law, and some who are violent and take the law into their own hands. And there are dishonest men and women who will do anything to get elected and once elected will be unfairly influenced by those who are powerful. And there are some who refuse to follow a law even though it was decided by a majority vote.

Don't let the idea of perfection ruin what is good.

Most of us will not be legislators or judges or police officers, so it can seem as though we as individuals have no responsibility for a lawful society. But everything we value – the ability to make choices, to create good character, to be free, to try for happiness and to live productive lives – is dependent on law and order. Without an orderly, lawful society, virtue becomes very difficult, and freedom is lost.

In your own way, and in accordance with your interests and talents, participate in making and upholding good government.

Some people are critical of our democratic system. Certainly it can be messy and distressing. But don't fall for the idea that because laws and politics aren't perfect they should be scorned. Inevitably there is disagreement, dispute and even chicanery. How could it be otherwise when there are so many ways of looking at things and not everyone is honest?

Everything starts someplace.

Don't waste a mistake. Learn from it.

THE ONLY WAY NEVER TO MAKE A MISTAKE IS TO DO NOTHING AND THAT IS A MISTAKE

Mistakes can teach us what not to do – the cat that sat on a hot stove never did that again – or they can point to a better way to do something. If they don't point directly, they can cause us to search for a better way.

When you have made a mistake, think over what led to the choice you made. Did you decide without enough information, take advice from someone who didn't know what he was talking about, submit to pressure, not follow through, fail to follow your core values, or not spend enough time and effort? Then decide whether or not to try the same thing again or to try something else.

We have to tolerate failure (without liking it) in order to move forward. People who can't admit failure, who always have to be right, get stuck. After all, if you're always right, what else is there to learn?

If you make a mistake that hurt someone, apologize. Don't make excuses or do a lot of explaining, just say you are sorry. If you have been thoughtless, try to make amends. If you have broken something, offer to replace it or have it fixed.

Try not to make really big mistakes that are hard to correct such as having an intimate relationship with someone who doesn't have good character, buying a house without having it inspected, or doing something illegal that could land you in jail. Some situations are very difficult to get out of.

Don't be ashamed that you were wrong yesterday
if you are wiser today.

Mistakes come in three sizes – small, medium, and large. Sometimes we have so much regret for a mistake we have made that there is no way to feel good. In such a case, we have to carry sorrow with us and go on. But we can begin to forgive ourselves by adding goodness to the world.

You are a child of the universe. You are worthy.

We can come out of trouble bitter or better.

Four of the most dangerous words in the world are, "Everyone is doing it."

WE CAN'T WANT TO GET ALONG SO MUCH THAT WE NEVER SAY NO

Sometimes friends and acquaintances put a lot of pressure on us to do something we don't want to do, or don't think is right, and we have to say no. Other times a person will try to shame us into doing something or will play on our sympathies, asking us to do something that is not our responsibility or that is against our values. (It is possible to have sympathy for someone without getting personally involved.)

There are tactful ways of saying no and rude ways. Tact is usually best, although sometimes you have to be insistent. You can tactfully say something like, "Thanks, but not now," or "I'll have to think about that," or "I'm not ready for that," or smile and change the subject; or you can think up your own polite, non-committal answer.

It's easy to think that you have to be rude in order for someone to listen to you when you say no, but this usually isn't true. There will be individuals who will try to intimidate you and force you or shame you into doing something. Or they may say they are offering a special deal that you would be a fool not to accept, or they may offer to give you something free, or say you owe it to them, or that you must do what they want because it is so important to them. Don't fall for this kind of manipulation. There are people who have no problem taking advantage of others, and you will meet your share of them.

Sometimes bravery is doing a difficult physical task.
Other times bravery is following your own values when
the values of others are not the same as yours.

Be tactful and polite when you say no. If you feel guilty, you are more likely to give in, stop saying no, and go along with someone who is pushing you to do something or buy something. Being polite and treating others decently is a way of taking care of yourself, because when you are polite and tactful you don't need to feel guilty for saying no.

Keep your cool even when someone is being pushy. Keep on saying no. Be brave.

Learn the ways of the world.

Ignorance = danger.

OPINIONS ARE LIKE FINGERPRINTS

THERE ARE A LOT OF THEM

One great problem in life is how to get along when there are differences of opinion. Do we argue and insist we are right? Do we call names or start a fight? Or do we respect the right of others to have an opinion and find ways to discuss our differences calmly? We can be polite when we disagree – even if only barely so.

It's natural to try to convince those who disagree with us that they are wrong. (Not everything natural is good, poison ivy isn't.) But the more a person is called wrong the more likely that person is to defend his or her position and insist that it is right. The best thing you can do when this happens is to say something like, "Could be, but I don't see it quite that way," without insisting that you are right. However, people who think that only one opinion can be right, and that the one they have is the right one, aren't easy to reason with. (This is how wars start.)

The thing is, opinions aren't facts. Opinions can be argued about, but they can't be proved. That the world is round is a fact that anyone can check out; that strawberries taste better than apples can't be proved. It is an opinion.

Because there are so many opinions, and because opinions can't be proved, some people think that there is no right or wrong in the world and that anything goes. They think that if badness or goodness can't be proved then all behaviors and beliefs are equal. This obviously is not true. Some things are better than others – much better. Societies that have fair laws and equal punishment for those who break the law are better places to live than those that do not. It is better to have money in our pockets than stones, better to be warm and dry than cold, wet and hungry, and better to be around those who are kind and honest than those who are mean and crooked.

Think for yourself and let others do the same.

The fact that not everyone agrees with us shouldn't change our values and beliefs. These are our opinions, and we stick with them because we think they are right, even though we may not be able to convince others.

There are people who think there is only one right opinion, that they know what it is, and that they have the right to use force against anyone who disagrees with them. But when we realize that opinions differ, and that this will always be so, we begin to understand why agreed upon laws and respect for individual rights must be our guides, not force.

On the big issues it helps if the people close to you have opinions and values similar to yours. There still will be plenty to disagree about. When you disagree, you can try to find a compromise, you can work out your differences over time, or agree to disagree. Or you can choose to part company.

If someone tells you that you are wrong, try not to say, "No, you are wrong!" You can try to convince others and others can try to convince you, but you have a life to live and better things to do than argue and fight. Some day you may change your opinion, but until you do, the one you have is the one you have. As long as it is lawful and doesn't harm others, you are entitled to it.

Good fortune comes and goes; persevere.

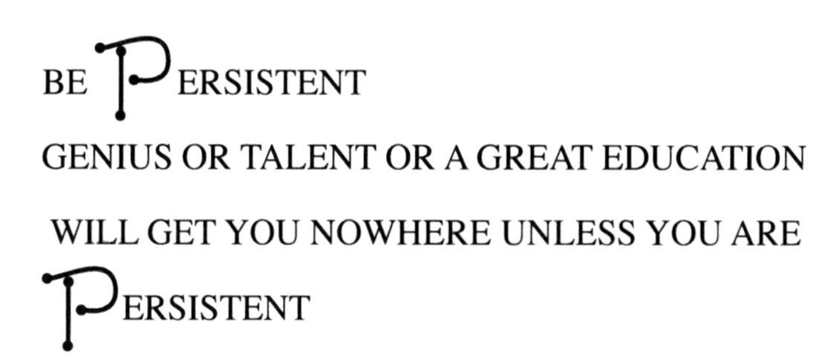

Persist, practice, and learn. Put your effort where your interests and talents are, where it will lead you only time will tell. When you meet obstacles, figure out how to get past them – learn more, get help, slow down and rest, or move faster. Don't give up.

After you choose a goal, keep at it until you reach it or until you are reasonably certain that nothing more can be gained, then change your goal and change your strategy – first, if possible, having planned what you will do next and how you will take care of yourself.

Persistence is a virtue, but like all good things, it can be carried to an extreme. In some situations it isn't wise to persist. If we don't make wise choices in choosing a job or in choosing a person to be with, it is important to make changes.

If you choose a course of study or a line of work and find it isn't what you thought it was, you can choose to change and start over. If you need to make a change, don't blame yourself, don't blame anyone else, and don't let your pride keep you from realizing that you made a mistake, even though this can be very hard to do. Pull up your socks and get on with it. When you find yourself in a hole, the thing to do is to stop digging.

Persist.

Keep on persisting.

But...

Sometimes stop persisting.

If you get involved with someone who turns out to be unreliable or who doesn't treat you well or whose values you don't agree with, give the situation a limited amount of time to change. If it doesn't change, move on if you can. If you make a similar mistake twice, slow down, take stock, and get good help to figure out how not to do it again. You're worth it.

Good things happen – bad things happen.

Keep on working for what is good.

If you question,
even only to yourself,
you won't easily be fooled
by fast talkers, flatterers,
and demagogues.

LOOK, LISTEN, QUESTION

Begin by noticing what is going on – how things look and what people say and do. Sometimes you have to guess but when possible, find out. Also question the answers you get. Some people act as though they know when they don't. As a general rule, actions are a better guide to understanding people than words.

Things keep changing; scientists make discoveries, people adopt new ideas, and things move faster and faster. But don't let change rob you of your values. Something new is not necessarily good nor does something old always need to be replaced. Don't discard what is old without reason or accept what is new without question. (Thoughtfulness and timeliness are old, but they haven't gone out of style or stopped being right.)

Not everyone likes being questioned, so be diplomatic and tactful when you ask. Don't ask personal questions and don't seem to be accusing someone of wrong doing or wrong thinking. You can say something like, "I've been thinking about the plan and about another option," rather than, "Why are we doing it this way?" And don't be surprised when someone takes offense at being questioned, even when you are tactful.

Better to ask twice than lose your way.

AVOID FOOLISH RISK

Risk is everywhere. No one can avoid it. From the time of getting up in the morning until going to bed at night, risk is part of being alive, but not all risk is equal. Some risks are big, some are small, and others are just plain foolish. It is foolish, for instance, to dive into water without knowing how deep it is – how deep it really is not how deep someone says it is. If it looks deep but isn't, and you jump or dive in, you might break your legs or crack your head open. To hope the water is deep enough when it isn't will get you into trouble. Taking a foolish risk can harm you beyond repair.

Before you do something risky, ask yourself, if this goes wrong, would the outcome be acceptable? Would cracking my head open be OK with me? When you ask yourself this question before taking a risk, you are guided by possible outcomes, not hope. (Hope is a great virtue, but it can be carried to an extreme, and a virtue carried to an extreme is no longer virtuous.)

We can't avoid all risk, but if we make thoughtful choices, we can avoid stupid risk. Be brave but don't be reckless.

Never take a dare. If someone dares you to do something unwise, say "Not today" or "I'm not THAT stupid."

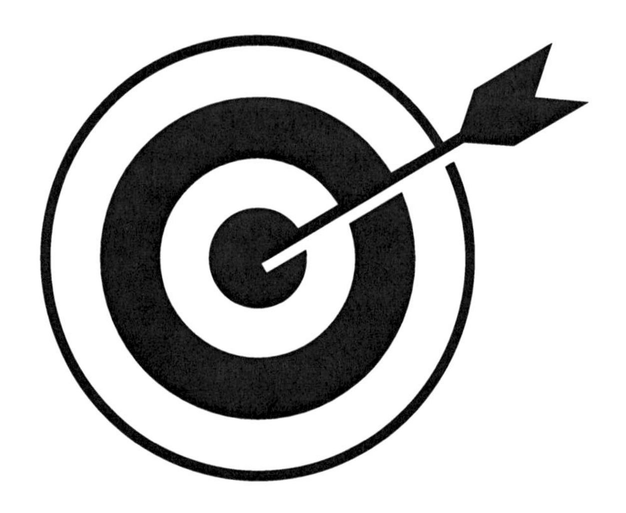

Some very smart people flunk life because they don't think ahead.

TO GET WHERE YOU WANT TO GO

YOU HAVE TO HAVE A

STRATEGY

You have to have a strategy to get where you want to be and to get what you want. No one will deliver the world to your doorstep or make your wishes come true. If you just hope for the best, not much is likely to happen – at least not much that you want to have happen.

Set a goal, have a plan, and keep changing it as you go along. Don't pay attention to someone who says you should stick with something you started if, in your best judgment, circumstances have changed.

Listen, ask questions and observe the strategy of others – what they do and what they don't do. What not to do is as important as what to do. You don't have to think up everything for yourself. The wheel has already been invented.

Your strategy can be to learn from people and from reading what others have written, or your strategy can be to meet people who could be helpful, or you can join organizations or take classes. You can also use strategy to avoid dangerous places and unreliable people and to get out of situations that have changed or that you don't agree with. Sometimes the best strategy is to just wait and watch.

Not everything is in our control. Unexpected events can interrupt any plan, so figure out what is in your control and what isn't.

Play the cards life gave you carefully and thoughtfully.

Without stepping on others or harming them, you need to make your own way in life. It may take awhile to make progress, but good things can take a long time.

Try not to worry about things over which you have no control but think how to steer clear of them and keep on going. And when circumstances are scary, talk to yourself and encourage yourself. Be thoughtful and optimistic. As much as you can, be in the driver's seat of your life.

And remember, everyone is more interested in himself or herself than in you.

Care what others think but don't let this be your only guide.

Thoughtfulness is a gift you can give.

BE THOUGHTFUL OF OTHERS

Pay attention to the feelings of people close to you. If someone's feelings are hurt or if a person is upset, don't say that it's wrong to feel that way. Feelings are feelings – it's what we do with them that matters.

When someone asks for advice, listen and try to see his or her point of view but give advice sparingly. Even when people ask for advice, they hardly ever really want it.

With someone outside your family that you see frequently, such as a neighbor, wave or call a greeting when you see them. If you need to talk with neighbors who aren't outside, call rather than going to the door, and call ahead before going to someone's house. At work or school or other places where you interact with people, mostly listen. Share parts of your life that aren't private but avoid getting personally involved. If someone tries to take advantage of your thoughtfulness by asking for a personal favor or personal attention that is inappropriate, politely back off and don't feel guilty for saying no.

Every situation with others involves some difficulty, in a family as much as anywhere. Some think that it's OK to stop treating others thoughtfully and decently in a family. They say, "After all, it's family. If I can't be real there, where can I?" But family is where there should be care, patience and appreciation, the place to be better than you are anywhere else.

Members of a family often are very different in outlook, personality, and talent. Getting along can be difficult. Sometimes one member of a family is not like any of the others. But whatever your differences,

We have to put up with a lot from others and they from us, but we shouldn't excuse meanness or dishonesty.

In some circumstances we may not be able to do or say anything about how others act, but in our own minds we shouldn't excuse bad behavior.

be loyal to your family members, don't share their secrets or talk against them to others. Be helpful when you can.

Sometimes one person in a family will be critical or bossy or try to get others to combine with them against another. It can be difficult to sort out feelings when this happens to you. In such situations some individuals put up without complaining. Others create a fuss and distance themselves, and some agree when they can, speak up when they need to defend themselves, but mostly go their own way. Sometimes nothing can be done except to keep your thoughts to yourself. However, there are times when something must be stopped.

It's hard to think that being treated harshly or thoughtlessly could be good in any way, but it can turn out in later years that problems made you stronger. Overcoming difficulties may help you have understanding and compassion for others and help you be strong when life is difficult.

Everyone wants to be cherished in someone's heart.

You get what you plant.

If you plant cabbage seeds, you don't get strawberries.

UGH – SOMETIMES WE DON'T WANT TO DO THINGS THAT ARE GOOD FOR US

We do some things we don't want to do because we like the results. We go to the dentist because we like the future with our own teeth, not false ones. We don't spend all our money so that we can take care of ourselves in an emergency. We are civil when we don't feel like it so that we don't offend others. We are honest so we can be trusted, and we obey the law so that we can keep our freedom. The easy, lazy way can sound good, but it seldom is.

Some people think that freedom means saying whatever they want to say or having whatever they want. They talk of their rights, and they see life as having unlimited opportunity for themselves with little obligation to others. But the belief that freedom is the right to do whatever pleases us ignores the fact that not all of our impulses are good and that some impulses and wishes need to be restrained. We are free to do all sorts of things, but unless we have control over the part of our nature that is selfish and bull-headed, we won't be happy, and we won't add goodness to the world.

You can't reach a goal by doing anything you feel like doing. If you want money in the bank, you have to spend less than you earn. If you want to be an engineer, you have to study and pass tests. If you want a happy, intimate relationship, there are things you must learn, things you must do, and things you must give up.

Goodness is a seed within you. Growing it is up to you.

And so it goes with everything except winning the lottery. But if you win the lottery and you haven't learned self-control, most likely the money soon will be gone and with it the freedom the money might have given you.

If you think you can have everything you want without applying limits, you will end up with nothing – or in trouble.

Self-expression is good. So is self-restraint.

Care for yourself by being careful who you trust.

VERIFY BEFORE YOU TRUST

Not everything you hear or read is accurate. A lot of what people say is opinion, not fact. Some individuals repeat things they have heard as though it is the truth, some make things up, some have strange ideas and some are ignorant or manipulative. Check things out for yourself by observing and asking questions. But be polite, there's no need to be rude or critical while you investigate an idea or a person.

You may meet someone who says, "Trust me," and if you question them and their ideas and don't do what they want you to do, they will accuse you of not being trustworthy. But trusting and being trustworthy are two different things. You have an obligation to be worthy of trust, but you are not obligated to trust everyone. Not everyone is worthy of trust. Some people don't have good values, and some are out to deceive, cheat, or get power over you.

In what you say and do, be trustworthy and honest. Your trustworthiness comes from what you do, not from following someone else.

Trust yourself more than you trust anyone else.

Don't trust someone who says, "It's OK. I've done it before."

Don't trust someone who says, "Trust me."

Don't trust someone who runs another person down and expects you to combine with them against that person.

Trust appropriately: trust your dentist to fix your teeth but not to take out your appendix.

Generally trust law officers and other authorities but always be cautious about trusting anyone, especially where your money and well-being are at stake.

Don't accept a "special deal" that you can get in on for a limited time.

Don't believe that love solves everything.

Don't buy something or agree to send money or give information to someone who calls, sends a message or knocks on the door.

Don't be too trusting. A bit of skepticism is a good thing.

Always read the fine print.

Maybe you will work hard and not reach

your goal; but if you don't work hard,

you know you won't.

WORK HARD AND PLAY BY THE RULES

If you are able to work, do your share. Anyone who expects a free ride in life will end up walking – or in the ditch. Become skilled and knowledgeable so you can earn your own way. Follow your interests and talents whether or not they will earn big money. All honest work is worthwhile.

If ill health or other circumstances take away your ability to work or to work as you had, your worth has not changed. It may feel like it, but it hasn't. There are still things you can do to add goodness to the world. You don't have to stop learning or caring.

In your work, aim for what you are fairly sure you can accomplish and keep aiming higher as you get better. (Don't try to jump a five-foot hurdle until you have jumped a one-foot hurdle.) And work smart. No matter how hard you try, you can't walk on water, but you can build a boat and travel on the water.

Try not to get discouraged. All good things are more complicated and take more time than seems possible. Don't put yourself down, even to yourself, but don't be so sure you are right that you can't accept helpful criticism or look realistically at yourself. When you make progress, even if it is small, give yourself credit.

Be alert for sudden events that can throw you off balance.

EXPECT THE BEST AND WORK FOR IT
BUT BE PREPARED FOR THE WORST

Life is full of many surprises, some good, some bad. Things come together, and they fall apart. To be prepared for the unexpected, keep some money set aside for emergencies, have health insurance and insurance to cover the loss of your possessions; and if others depend on you, have life insurance. At work and in your personal life, allow extra time so you can catch up if something throws you off balance. Be thoughtful of others so if you need help the kindness may be returned.

When things go well, be full of grace and modesty. When things don't go well, keep on being full of grace and modesty. No one can win all the time.

When you are successful, be proud and happy but don't brag. Success is wonderful, and hopefully adds goodness to the world, but it doesn't make you better than others. You can be pleased with your accomplishments without being arrogant.

Some individuals think only of themselves and aren't interested in any success but their own. They spend time bragging about themselves and putting others down. People aren't always what we want them to be or what they seem to be or claim to be. They are what they are.

People wrapped up in themselves make small packages.

Sometimes we act correctly with the best knowledge we have and still suffer defeat or are disliked by others. It is foolish to think we will never be hurt, never lose, or never be betrayed. Life can really, really hurt. But in all the difficulty life brings, we can be proud of persevering, being honest, caring for others and not harming others. Whatever happens, keep on believing in yourself and in the value of life. Treat others decently, be kind, care for the day.

Things *can be taken away from us, but good deeds and acts of virtue never can be.*

Praise the world – praise life – be grateful.

YOU CREATE YOUR OWN CHARACTER

In planning our lives and setting goals, we think of what we want to do and what we want to have. Maybe being a scientist sounds good, or an explorer, an inventor, a writer, a farmer, an engineer, or a lawyer. Living a simple life may sound good or living in the city may be appealing. There are so many ideas about what to do because we are unique individuals with different talents, ideas, values and hopes.

Some of us will have great adventures or become rich and famous, but most of us will live quiet lives – which if they are unselfish, kind, and honest probably will add as much to the world as the lives of those who become famous. You don't need to have your name in the history books to have added goodness to the world.

If you can develop the talents you were born with and develop good character, you will have done what you were meant to do.

Not that developing good character is something easy or automatic that just happens like growing taller as children do. It isn't easy because we aren't born either good or bad, or knowing anything about the world, or how it works, or anything about good and evil.

Knowing how to do things and learning the meaning of things comes gradually and with experience. This is why infants and children must be treated with the greatest kindness and care and why we must be patient as we teach them the difference between goodness and badness. Developing good character takes learning and practice and self-control.

There will always be someone who is better looking and
has more money and talent than you.
There also will be someone who has less or
who is not so good looking.
Settle into who you are and do your best.

So how do you create good character?

You actually create your character by the ***choices*** you make and with the ***actions*** that follow your choices. One after another, after another, they add up. In all this round, beautiful, awesome, fearful world, only we human beings can do this – only we can choose between this or that. The ability to choose is our great privilege and our great responsibility.

You may make choices that are not wise or that seemed wise when you made them but that don't work out, and perhaps you will be furious with yourself or even depressed. It sometimes happens that no matter what choice you make, circumstance or luck intervene and cause you to stumble or even knock you down. Life can be very difficult. We may wish life was easy, but it is what it is, sometimes sad, disappointing, and scary but sometimes glorious and full of greatness and meaning.

As you create your own character, be patient with yourself without being smug. Believe in the spark of eternity that is in you (and in every human soul) – a spark that doesn't have anything to do with what you have done, how you look, what you have, or who your parents were. It came with you when you were born into the adventure of life.

The light of eternity is always within you, but you have to make it shine. There is goodness in you to start with, but you have to ***become*** good by the choices you make and by what you say and do. This is not a contradiction – you are good, AND you must become good.

And as you go along your path in life, making choices, deciding what to do, and creating yourself, believe that beyond what it is possible to know and understand in this imperfect world, there is good will, love, and meaning – a light and high beauty beyond the passing clouds – a reality that transcends the confusion of this world.

It's not only what and when you do something,

but how you do it.

We are born with bodies, but creating character is a

"do-it-yourself" project – the job of a lifetime.

Civilization is victory over chaos.

It must be won over and over again.

CIVILIZATION CAN'T EXIST WITHOUT RULES

In a game there are rules and anyone who wants to play must follow the rules. Anyone who doesn't follow the rules will be penalized, and anyone who keeps on not following the rules will be kicked out of the game.

It's the same in a civilized community. People choose rules for how to live together, or accept the rules their community has decided on in the past. These rules set out what is acceptable behavior and what is unacceptable. Without rules and laws individuals will do whatever they feel like doing, or invent new rules for themselves, or do whatever is convenient. The result is chaos.

We need rules because we aren't born with innate knowledge of how best to act and how to do things. Unlike animals, we don't have instincts that determine our actions. Birds don't have to be taught how to fly south in the winter, or how to make nests, or how to care for their young, and bears don't have to be taught how and when to hibernate. But we human beings aren't born understanding life or even how to care for ourselves. We learn how to live from those around us and from our experiences.

It takes a long time to grow up, because there is so much to learn.

Although rules and laws differ in various cultures, almost without exception they will be concerned with property rights, methods of containing violence, regulation of sexual desires, and appropriate ways of treating others, including children and the old.

Without civilization we are pretty much nothing.

But even when there are rules, not everyone will follow them. Some will try to get more than their fair share – robbing, lying and cheating, saying "I'm right, you're wrong!" They refuse to accept what the majority has fairly and openly decided and try to blackmail others into doing what they want. And there will be disagreement as to what the rules should be. But when there are laws and rules, and if the penalties for breaking the rules are fair, and if the people have a part in deciding what the rules and laws are, each person can lead his or her life's journey in community with others.

We can't do without other people, even though at times we hardly know what to do with them.

The people of the past made the present possible, and we make civilization possible, now and in the future.

Where you are is the place to start.

Carry On

With Love to all
Paul

Sara and Sam Maitree are writers who live in the Midwest.

CPSIA information can be obtained at www.ICGtesting.com
Printed in the USA
LVOW07s0759111114

413068LV00003B/3/P

9 781600 479823